<The Power of CODING/>

The Power
of Python

Rachel Keranen

Cavendish
Square
New York

Published in 2018 by Cavendish Square Publishing, LLC
243 5th Avenue, Suite 136, New York, NY 10016

Library of Congress Cataloging-in-Publication Data

Names: Keranen, Rachel.
Title: The power of python / Rachel Keranen.
Description: New York : Cavendish Square Publishing, 2018. | Series: The
power of coding | Includes bibliographical references and index.
Identifiers: ISBN 9781502629487 (library bound) |
ISBN 9781502634153 (pbk.) | ISBN 9781502629494 (ebook)
Subjects: LCSH: Python (Computer program language)--Juvenile
literature. | Microcomputers--Programming--Juvenile literature.
Classification: LCC QA76.73.P98 K47 2018 | DDC 005.13/3--dc23

Editorial Director: David McNamara
Editor: Caitlyn Miller
Copy Editor: Rebecca Rohan
Associate Art Director: Amy Greenan
Designer: Joe Parenteau
Production Coordinator: Karol Szymczuk
Photo Research: J8 Media

The photographs in this book are used by permission and through the courtesy of: Cover
Hero Images Inc./Alamy Stock Photo; p. 4 AF Archive/Alamy Stock Photo; p. 7 U.S. Army/
Wikimedia Commons/File:Two women operating ENIAC (full resolution).jpg/CC PD; p. 8
Computer Laboratory, University of Cambridge/Wikimedia Commons/File:EDSAC (25).jpg/
CC BY-SA 2.0; p. 17 BestVectorIcon/Shutterstock.com; p. 20 Austin McKinley/Wikimedia
Commons/File:Google Campus, Mountain View, CA.jpg/CC BY-SA 3.0; p. 21 Geek3/
Wikimedia Commons/File:Matplotlib screenshot.png/CC BY-SA 3.0; p. 31 Darcy Padilla/
Wikimedia Commons/File:Brendan Eich Mozilla Foundation official photo.jpg/CC BY-SA 3.0;
p. 32 Daniel Stroud/Wikimedia Commons/File:Guido-portrait-2014.jpg/CC BY-SA 4.0; p. 40
kay roxby/Shutterstock.com; p. 41 Eric Isselee/Shutterstock.com; p. 43 peterfactors/Shutterstock.
com; p. 47 IB Photography/Shutterstock.com; p. 49 NASA/Wikimedia Commons/File:Chandra
X-ray Observatory (transparent).png/CC PD; p. 51 NASA/Wikimedia Commons/File:Cosmic
'Winter' Wonderland.jpg/CC PD; p. 54 Annette Shaff/Shutterstock.com; p. 57 Eric S Raymond
and company/Wikimedia Commons/File:Eric S Raymond portrait.jpg/CC BY-SA 2.0; p. 59
TACstock1/Shutterstock.com; p. 62 EggHeadPhoto/Shutterstock.com; p. 63 Joel Holdsworth/
Wikimedia Commons/File:Feynmann Diagram Gluon Radiation.svg/CC BY-SA 3.0; p. 69
NetPhotos/Alamy Stock Photo; p. 76 Solis Images/Shutterstock.com; p. 79 Quinn Dombrowski/
Flickr/CC BY-SA 2.0; p. 81 Duncan Hull/Flickr/CC BY-SA 2.0; p. 86 jejim/Shutterstock.
com; p. 95 Zapp2Photo/Shutterstock.com; p. 98 Quality Stock Arts/Shutterstock.com.

Printed in the United States of America

The History of Python

Python is one of the most popular computer-programming languages and also one of the most versatile. It can be used in web development, scientific computing, **data science**, game development, film animation, and more. Before diving into the history of Python, however, it's worth exploring what exactly a programming language is. Understanding more about the field of programming gives context for why coding languages exist and why people continue to develop new ones, like a Dutch programmer named Guido van Rossum did in 1989 when he invented Python.

Opposite: Python is named after the sketch comedy show *Monty Python's Flying Circus*. The email term "spam" also came from a Monty Python sketch in which a restaurant put Spam (canned meat) in every dish.

A Brief History of Computer Programming

A programming language is a language that provides a way for humans to give instructions to computers. Programming languages take instructions given in a language that humans can understand (such as Python) and translate those instructions into a format that machines can understand. Humans could correspond directly with machines if desired, and this was actually how it worked when computer programming first began.

First Computers, First Code

The first general-purpose computer was ENIAC, or the Electronic Numerical Integrator And Computer. ENIAC was built by a professor and graduate student from the Moore School of Engineering between 1943 and 1945. ENIAC's construction occurred during World War II, and the United States government recognized the value of a machine that could make rapid arithmetic calculations (such as for determining weapons' trajectories) and financed the project.

ENIAC was completed in 1945, just after the war had ended. It had value in many other arenas, however, such as nuclear physics and engineering. To use ENIAC, programmers had to enter instructions by plugging in wires. Each wire plugged in represented a single instruction, and there could be thousands of

ENIAC's first programmers were six women, called computers, from the Moore School of Electrical Engineering at the University of Pennsylvania.

instructions for solving a single math problem. Thus, once the machine was configured for a problem, ENIAC's programmers usually kept that configuration for a few weeks before rewiring it to solve a new type of problem. ENIAC's invention is widely considered to be the beginning of the digital era.

In 1946, an early computer scientist named John von Neumann proposed that instructions should be stored inside the computer and that programs should be written in binary code to represent the two possible states of electronic circuits: on or off. (His proposal inspired the design of the Electronic Delay Storage Automatic Calculator, EDSAC, built at Cambridge University and first operated in 1949.) Binary code is

EDSAC first ran on May 6, 1949, and was in service for more than nine years before being replaced by EDSAC 2.

written using series of 1s and 0s and was a considerable improvement from the days-long wiring process required to program ENIAC. However, binary code is still challenging for most humans to write and edit.

Binary code is considered low-level code because it represents the state of computer circuits and thus the language of the machine itself. It is also often referred to as a first-generation programming language. Early computer programmers entered binary code by using punch cards or punch tape or by flipping switches on the computer itself.

Compilers and Interpreters

In 1949, a pioneering computer scientist and United States Navy Admiral named Grace Hopper invented a

compiler that allowed programmers to use **mnemonics** that represented commonly used chunks of code called **subroutines**. The mnemonics were symbolic code that the compiler translated back into those commonly used subroutines. For example, the line of assembly code "LOOP: MOV.B r0, #80 ;initialise counter" translates to and corresponds directly to the binary code 11 0000 1000 0000, which the computer understands. While the assembly code is not entirely intuitive, it does use English words that are more comprehensible than the 1s and 0s of binary code. The resulting programs ran more slowly because of the compiling step, but they were much easier to write.

Hopper advocated creating a programming language written entirely in English, but she was told that computers couldn't understand English. Nonetheless, Hopper invented a new compiler that translated twenty English-language commands related to business into language the UNIVAC computers she worked with could understand. Hopper also gave us the term "debug" for eliminating errors after finding a dead moth inside a Mark II computer that was preventing the computer from accurately reading the paper tape-based program input. These mnemonic-based programming languages, also called assembly code, were considered the second generation of programming.

By the end of the 1950s, computers were still expensive machines used mostly by businesses and research organizations, but programming languages had advanced into a third generation. The third generation of programming languages, which began with languages such as COBOL, FORTRAN, and BASIC, began to look more like English. COBOL was created to simplify business-oriented data processing, FORTRAN was designed to simplify scientific computing, and BASIC was invented to make a general-purpose language that was approachable for beginners. Hopper's compiler was a precursor to COBOL, a language that she also helped create.

These languages were more abstract than the first two generations of computer programming languages, which is to say that they were less like machine language and more like English. Increased abstraction was a significant improvement for programmers because it increased both the ease of programming and the readability of the code. (FORTRAN, COBOL, and BASIC are all still in use today, though most programmers generally prefer more modern languages such as C, Java, or Python.)

As languages grew more abstract, there became an increasingly important role for the intermediate technologies that understand the human input (high-level code) and can translate it to the computer language (machine language). This intermediary can either be a compiler, as Hopper had invented, or an **interpreter**.

A compiler is a computer program that converts other high-level computer programs into machine code that can be executed by a computer. Typically, a program is compiled before it is run. An interpreter is a computer program that provides a similar function through a different process. An interpreter skips the compilation step and translates high-level code, one line at a time, into an intermediate form that the computer can execute.

When someone creates a new programming language, they are essentially building either a new compiler or a new interpreter program. Typically, the new language is built using a pre-existing computer programming language. Most of the time, someone creates a new computer programming language because they have identified flaws in existing languages or they want functionality that does not yet exist.

Python, a high-level interpreter program that emerged shortly after the birth of the internet, was created largely to address shortcomings in existing languages. Today, Python is widely used by huge entities such as Google and NASA as well as small tech startups. Python's start, however, began about thirty years ago when Guido van Rossum was working in the Netherlands at a company named CWI: the Centrum Wiskunde & Informatica (the Center for Mathematics and Computer Science.)

The Birth of Python

In the late 1980s, van Rossum worked as a programmer at CWI, the Netherland's national research institute for mathematics and computer science. Programmers at CWI had previously designed a computer programming language called ABC. ABC was a general-purpose programming language, which means that it could be used for a variety of purposes instead of a single niche need. CWI programmers created the language to replace BASIC. BASIC was well known because it was the programming language that came installed on personal computers like the Apple II and the Commodore 64, and it had been in use for decades. BASIC stood for "Beginner's All-Purpose Symbolic Instruction Code" and was designed to be easy for beginners to use. By the mid-1980s, it was beginning to be replaced by new languages like Pascal and, potentially, ABC.

Like BASIC, ABC could be used for everyday programming. It was also an interactive programming language, meaning that the programmer can write, modify, and run code in the same window. These qualities made it a good choice for rapid prototyping, or quickly building a model of something for testing and validation. Its interactive nature also made it a good fit for teaching because an instructor could demonstrate a concept, work through code examples, and run code in a single window. The ABC programming language never took off, however. After a few years, work on the project was terminated.

Project Amoeba

Van Rossum had been one of the programmers who worked on the ABC team. After the ABC project was shut down, he moved to a project called Amoeba, which CWI was working on in partnership with the Vrije Universiteit Amsterdam. Amoeba's goal was to build a distributed operating system, which makes a network of many computers appear to act as a single machine. For example, a program can be run on one computer in the network and access data from any other computer in the network.

The Amoeba team felt they needed a high-level programming language that would be easier and faster to develop in than C. C is a powerful language that is fast to run, and it's still commonly used today. However, it is not an easy language for many beginner programmers. The need for a language that was more programmer friendly became one of the inspirations for van Rossum's work on Python. In describing the beginning of Python, he writes:

It occurred to me that a scripting language with a **syntax** like ABC but with access to the Amoeba system calls would fill the need. I realized that it would be foolish to write an Amoeba-specific language, so I decided that I needed a language that was generally extensible. During the 1989 Christmas holidays, I had a lot of time on my hands, so I decided to give it a try.

Van Rossum kept what he liked of ABC, and when it came to things he didn't like, he did the opposite. Often, in those cases, he turned to the C language to find inspiration. In fact, the Python interpreter itself is written in C. Over the next year, the Amoeba team used van Rossum's new language and gave feedback that helped improve the language and shape its early development.

Van Rossum named his new language Python, a name that references the popular British comedy sketch series *Monty Python's Flying Circus*, which was broadcast on BBC television. Van Rossum believes that the name was unintentionally a component in the language's early popularity—the pop culture associations helped Python stand out from other programming languages.

Hitting It Big

In February 1991, van Rossum shared Python on Usenet, a bulletin board-like discussion site that was a precursor to the World Wide Web. Usenet was organized by subject into collections of posts called newsgroups, and van Rossum posted Python in a newsgroup called alt.sources. Alt.sources was a repository for source code (the code for a computer program) that people wanted to distribute and share with others.

One major difference between Python's launch and ABC's launch was the existence of a new invention: the internet. The internet, coupled with advances in computer science, had changed the way computer-software creators and users interacted. Before the internet was available, there was a much longer lag time between the release of a software product and feedback from users. After the internet became available to the public, a software user could share a question and receive a nearly immediate answer. Likewise, a creator could ask for input or opinions on their product and receive nearly immediate feedback. The easy back-and-forth and the general ease of communicating and sharing ideas were factors in Python's early success.

In March of 1993, programmers excited about Python created a comp.lang.python newsgroup on Usenet. A year and a half later, in November 1994, van Rossum conducted the first Python workshop in the United States. About twenty people attended this first workshop.

It's difficult to track how many people use Python today because Python is free to download and comes already installed on many computers. However, based on download rates and other metrics, it's generally thought that around one million programmers use Python to store information, analyze huge amounts of data, build web applications and **application programming interfaces (APIs)**, and more.

An API is a set of standards for how one application can talk to another application. For example, the Twitter API makes it possible to write a tweet about an article you're reading, right from the article itself. In June 2013, Python won a prestigious national award in the Netherlands, the Dutch COMMIT/, which recognized the pioneering work and worldwide adoption of the language among individuals and large organizations alike.

A core development team, which van Rossum leads, continues to develop new features for the language. Van Rossum is responsible for shaping the evolution of the language and making ultimate decisions about its direction when needed. Within the Python community, van Rossum carries the affectionate title of "Benevolent Dictator for Life," another reference to Monty Python.

Python's Evolution

Though the inspiration for Python was Amoeba, a deeply technical project related to operating systems

APIs help applications communicate with each other. Hundreds of thousands of programmers use Python to build APIs.

and computer networks, when van Rossum began creating Python, he wanted to create a language that could be used for more than one specific project. Today, Python lives up to its "general purpose" description and is used in a variety of ways.

Many web developers use Python to build web applications. Google, for example, uses Python extensively to build its massively popular web applications including YouTube. Python is also used heavily in data science, which describes a range of industries and roles where professionals work with huge amounts of data to find patterns and meaningful trends. For example, many people wear fitness devices such as FitBits or carry a motion-sensing smartphone

Guido van Rossum

○ ○ ○

One of Guido van Rossum's first encounters with programming was at age ten when his parents gave him an educational electronics kit that he used to design his own circuits and build electronics models. In a 2016 speech, van Rossum described himself as follows:

> Let me introduce myself. I'm a nerd, a geek. I'm probably somewhere on the autism spectrum. I'm also a late bloomer. I graduated from college when I was twenty-six. I was forty-five when I got married. I'm now sixty years old, with a fourteen-year-old son. Maybe I just have a hard time with decisions ...
>
> I took one of my first electronics models, a blinking light, to show and tell in fifth grade. It was a total dud—nobody cared or understood its importance. I think that's one of my earliest memories of finding myself a geek: until then I had just been a quiet, quick learner.

In high school, van Rossum enjoyed electronics and physics and worked hard at academics. After graduating high school, he attended the University of Amsterdam. It was there that he received a bachelor's degree in mathematics and a master's degree in mathematics and computer science. It was also at the University of Amsterdam that van Rossum fell in love with computer programming.

While in university, van Rossum began spending time in the basement of the science building, which contained a mainframe computer. Mainframe computers are computers used by large organizations such as universities or corporations to run important applications and conduct huge amounts of data processing. They were originally built within large cabinets called mainframes. Van Rossum was fascinated by the computer and quickly learned to build programs for it in languages that were popular at the time, including ALGOL, FORTRAN, and Pascal.

He became part of a community of students and staff who spent their time around the computer sharing programs and subroutines. Time on the computer was highly competitive, and van Rossum was excited when he saw a posting for a job working with the mainframe computer's operating system group. It meant he could have more time with the computer. The job slowed down his progress toward completing his degree, but he loved the work.

When van Rossum graduated, he began working at CWI on the ABC team. After leaving CWI in 1995, he moved to the United States, where he got married and had a son. He has worked at a variety of software companies in the United States including Google and Dropbox, his current company. He spends 50 percent of his work time developing the Python language. In 2002, Van Rossum received the Free Software Foundation Award for his work on Python.

Google's campus, called the Googleplex, has a variety of services for employees, including fitness classes and massages.

that tracks steps throughout the day. The makers of those devices hire data scientists to study the huge amounts of movement data gathered from millions of users to find patterns and help the company optimize their products or services.

Google uses Python in this capacity as well, using the language to analyze data and optimize the ability for apps like Gmail to spot spam emails. You also see this in action any time suggestions for how to complete a search phrase appear in the search bar. If you and a few friends type in the beginning of a search phrase, you might all get different suggestions. Google's algorithms try to predict what you'll like based on your region as well as things you've searched for in the past.

For similar reasons, Python is also very popular amongst academic scientists. Scientists typically gather huge amounts of data while conducting research. For example, a seismologist might have spreadsheets filled with near-constant seismic readings taken by tens or hundreds of seismometers placed along a tectonic fault line. This data needs to be processed and put into charts and scatter plots and other forms to be meaningful to scientists. Python has many high-quality data science **packages** that make that processing possible. In Python, a package is a collection of code files containing common functionality that programmers can use in their applications. Packages are synonymous with libraries, a common term for the same concept in other programming languages.

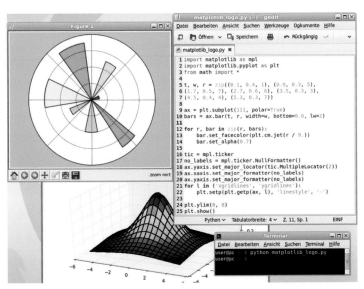

Python source code files can be used to create visual representations of data.

Web Development Frameworks

A big advancement in the use of Python was the creation of Python-specific web development frameworks. A web development framework is a tool programmers use to build websites faster and with better design and functionality. Using a web framework is something like using a coloring book instead of drawing from scratch. Both approaches can result in a beautiful picture, but the coloring book makes the process quicker and easier and accessible to people of varying experience levels.

A web framework is like the outline of a drawing. Web frameworks consist of packages and **modules** (Python source-code files) that streamline and standardize the development process. These modules typically automate or simplify creating models for retrieving and showing data based on application user requests, ways to create an account and log in and out of that account, ways to upload files, and other requests common to most web applications.

The most commonly used Python web framework is Django. Django was originally created in July of 2005 by the web department of a newspaper in Lawrence, Kansas. Today, it is an open-source project (which means it's free to use, modify, and share) that is run by an international team of volunteers.

The intent of Django is to make web development "ridiculously fast," "reassuringly secure," and "exceedingly scalable" according to the Django website. It's faster because some of the decisions and configuration are done for the programmer by the framework. It's "reassuringly" secure because those preset configurations were selected with security in mind. Security is an enormous concern in web development, as is evidenced each time a company reveals that it has accidentally leaked thousands of credit card numbers or Social Security numbers due to hacking. Better security makes it harder for hackers to access stored data. Django is also designed to be scalable, so it can support a website with small amounts of traffic and then ramp up to support heavier traffic as a company grows.

Django's core principles are to automate as much development as possible and to adhere to the DRY principle of software development. DRY stands for "Don't Repeat Yourself," and it states that there should be no unnecessary repetition of code in a program. Django is a full-**stack** framework—it includes all the components including the deeply technical, behind-the-scenes elements of building a web application.

Django is the most popular Python web framework, but it is not the only framework available. The second-most popular Python web framework is Flask, which bills itself as a microframework for Python, based in part on "good intentions." A microframework is essentially a less-extensive web development framework. Flask provides the base application server needed to build a web application as well as some additional components. Compared to Django, many more elements of web application development are left to the individual programmer to set up.

Implementations of Python

There are two meanings of the word "Python" when talking about computers. The first meaning is the language itself. The second is the program that comes installed on a computer or that is available for download via the official Python Software Foundation website.

Since Python was first developed by van Rossum, other programmers have created new **implementations** of Python. This means that the programmers have a new Python interpreter (the second definition) which uses the same Python language **specification** (the first definition) as the traditional implementation.

A programming language specification defines the rules of a programming language so that people who use that language have a shared understanding of how to read and write it. Often, there is an official document that defines the specification of a computer programming language. Other times, the specification is defined by example. In Python's case, there is an official Python specification published on the Python Software Foundation website.

An implementation of a programming language refers to the interpreter or compiler that you use when you install a programming language onto your computer. The standard implementation of Python can simply be called Python, but it is often called CPython to distinguish it from newer, specialized implementations.

When the core Python team makes a change to the language, the change is made to the CPython implementation. Over time, however, other programmers have made their own implementations of Python including Jython, IronPython, and PyPy. These new implementations are examples of new interpreters that use the Python language specification.

Jython is designed to integrate the clear syntax of Python into the high-performance Java programming platform. Similarly, IronPython integrates with Microsoft's .NET framework.

PyPy runs on a Just-in-Time (JIT) compiler that compiles PyPy code into machine code at the time of program **execution**. JIT compilers are a hybrid of compilers (which compile code before the program is run) and interpreters (which translate code at runtime). PyPy's JIT compiler makes it much faster than standard Python. PyPy also tends to use less memory when running Python programs compared to the CPython implementation. Van Rossum is frequently quoted as having said, "If you want your code to run faster, you should probably just use PyPy."

Python 2 Versus Python 3

Programming languages, like smartphones and computers, receive continual updates to strengthen and improve them. In 2008, van Rossum and the core team of Python developers released a pivotal new version of Python. It was called Python 3, and it majorly overhauled the previous version of Python, Python 2.6.

Typically, new releases of a software language or application clean up bugs and introduce new features, but they also maintain backward compatibility. This means that a new version of a software product is able to use the same interfaces (the visual component of an application that a user sees) and data as older versions did. If you've ever installed a new update of your smartphone's operating system, it almost certainly maintained backward compatibility with the older versions of the operating system.

For example, updating from iOS 10.2 to iOS 10.3 on an iPhone introduced new features such as the ability to use the "Find My iPhone" feature to find Apple's Bluetooth headphones, AirPods. All of the old functionality was there as well. The native clock app was still there, your calendar app still contained your upcoming events, and photos that you took when you had iOS 10.2 installed were still there and able to be edited, shared, and deleted.

This is the typical expected behavior when a new version of software comes out. And yet, when Python 3 came out, it broke backward compatibility with Python 2. Furthermore, the core team announced that the last-ever release of a Python 2-based version of the language would be Python 2.7. Eventually, Python 2.7 will not be supported by the Python core development team, and all Python users will have to use Python 3 to receive new updates and bug fixes.

Python 3's release was a big deal within the Python community because it meant that companies that used Python had to decide to either update their existing code or use code that would eventually no longer be supported. The obvious choice is to eventually "port" or adapt all of the Python 2 code to Python 3 code. For large companies with a lot of Python 2 code, this was a big task, and not all have done it yet.

The biggest difference between the two versions is that Python 3 has better Unicode support. Unicode is an international encoding system that assigns a unique number to every character to unify how text-based data is ultimately represented in numeric form. All

A Dutch Innovation Hub

○ ○ ○

World War II lasted from 1939 to 1945 and involved nearly every region of the world. Tens of millions of people died, and Europe was left in shambles. Cities had been leveled by bombs, homes were destroyed, farms suffered severe losses of people and commodities, and transportation systems had been demolished or dismantled. As the war faded, it was clear there had to be a significant rebuilding effort to help Europe recover from the war.

As part of the rebuilding effort, the Dutch government founded the Centrum Wiskunde & Informatica, or CWI, in 1946 as a national research institute that could help advance the country's postwar reconstruction. CWI's staff quickly began contributing with significant technological advancements.

Early on, for example, CWI scientists developed the first computers in the Netherlands, including the ARRA computer in 1952. In the 1950s, CWI also performed the calculations for the Delta Works, a series of dams built at the delta region where the Rhine, Meuse, and Sheldt rivers meet the North Sea. Over one-third of the Netherlands is below sea level, and flooding has historically been a significant problem. More than 1,800 people died from a massive flood in 1953, and the Delta Works project was launched to control flooding in the region. The Delta Works dams took decades to build. When completed, they reduced flooding in the region and improved the water quality as well. The Delta Works project is such an accomplishment that some people consider it to be the eighth world wonder.

In 1988, CWI became the birthplace of the European internet when it became the first non-American organization to connect to NSFNET, or the National Science Foundation Network. NSFNET was a network founded in 1985 to link researchers to the powerful computing resources at supercomputer centers located at Princeton, the University of California San Diego, the University of Illinois at Urbana-Champaign, Cornell University, and the Pittsburgh Supercomputing Center. NSFNET became one of several government-funded computer-networking groups that led to the modern internet. It took significant negotiations for CWI to gain access, but soon other academic and research organizations were connected as well.

In 1986, CWI also registered one of the first country-specific internet domains in the world: .nl.

CWI is still going strong today. The goal of the organization is to discover and develop new ideas that benefit society. They employ dozens of researchers, postdocs (recent PhD graduates), and PhD students from over twenty-five countries. Recent CWI projects include developing proactive planning methods for emergency responders (such as paramedics and fire crews), investigating smart energy networks, and modeling and simulating phenomena such as lightning, ocean currents, and proteins.

major software companies have adopted the Unicode Standard, including Apple, IBM, Microsoft, and Oracle. There were also some changes to Python's syntax, such as replacing the print **statement** (which displays text) to a print **function** (which also displays text but uses different syntax). There were changes to how errors are displayed, as well as how division is calculated. If you are considering learning to program in Python, it is better to choose books, tutorials, and other resources that focus on Python 3.

Influence of Python

Python made a strong impact on subsequent general-purpose programming languages. JavaScript, the programming language that gives web pages both elegance and interactivity, for example, was strongly impacted by Python. JavaScript was created in 1995 by Brendan Eich, who also cofounded the Mozilla Foundation and the Mozilla Corporation. When Eich was designing the JavaScript specification, called ECMAScript, he looked to Python for inspiration. He wanted to reuse the developer knowledge honed from years of Python development instead of starting from scratch.

A programming language even more heavily influenced by Python is Boo, which adopted elements of Python's style guide, syntax, and **object** model.

In programming, objects are a type of data structure. Boo, however, was more closely integrated with Microsoft's .NET programming framework.

The Groovy programming language was created as an effort to combine the Python design philosophy and elements of the Java programming language. Groovy has the

Brendan Eich, the creator of JavaScript

processing-speed advantages of Java but incorporates elements of the Python design philosophy.

Success through Simplicity

Python has been a popular language used in various different industries for over three decades. One of the language's biggest strengths is the ease and speed of programming. That's largely because the Python language is simple and straightforward. A beginning programmer can pick up Python much more quickly than a language such as C or Java while still accomplishing many of the same goals. Even an experienced programmer can typically program more quickly in Python than in languages such as C or Java. In the next chapter, we'll look more closely at Python code and how it works.

<Chapter Two/>

How It Works

There are dozens of different programming languages that a programmer can choose to use for software development. Some are highly specialized and have narrow use cases, such as R, which is designed for statistical computing and graphics. It wouldn't make sense to use R to develop a web or mobile application. It also wouldn't make sense to use R to develop an operating system. However, it makes perfect sense to use R for analyzing financial market data or geospatial data.

There are many general-purpose programming languages, however, that can be used to accomplish all

Opposite: Python creator Guido van Rossum

of the goals mentioned above. C, which was initially developed between 1969 and 1973, is an example of an early, general-purpose programming language that is still widely used today. Python, Ruby, and Java are all examples of general-purpose programming languages that appeared one after the other in the 1990s. In many use cases, any one of these languages would suffice. Yet people kept inventing new languages when there were already languages that worked. In a 2016 speech, Guido van Rossum offered his perspective on this perpetual innovation:

> Typically when you ask a programmer to explain to a lay person what a programming language is, they will say that it is how you tell a computer what to do. But if that was all, why would they be so passionate about programming languages when they talk among themselves?
>
> In reality, programming languages are how programmers express and communicate *ideas*—and the audience for those ideas is other programmers, not computers. The reason: the computer can take care of itself, but programmers are always working with other programmers, and poorly communicated ideas can cause expensive flops.

There are many programming languages that can accomplish the same general goals. However, some programming languages are better designed to allow programmers to express and communicate ideas. Van Rossum himself was very intentional in how he designed Python.

Design Ethos

Some programming languages are built around the idea that there are many ways to do something. Python, however, takes an opinionated stance. One of the most famous tenets of Python is that there is usually one obviously correct way to do something.

A Python core developer named Tim Peters captured this tenet along with other defining principles of Python in "The Zen of Python," which is posted on the Python Software Foundation website. A good summary of Peters's treatise might be something like this: ideas that are simply and clearly stated are better than ideas that are complicated or confusing.

Another defining Python design principle mentioned in the "Zen of Python" is that code must be easy to read. In the process of designing software, there is significant emphasis on having someone review code for quality before it goes into production (called code review). Likewise, it's necessary to dedicate time to reading existing code before modifying or adding to it. Thus, code is typically read more frequently than it is written.

With this balance in mind, there is a Python style guide that states how Python should be written and formatted. Following the style guide provides consistency within programs and within teams of programmers working with the same code.

According to the Python style guide, white space has meaning in Python. (White space is the blank space surrounding text or images, such as the white space framing the text of this book.) This is not common in other languages. In Python, you can look at a program and, from its shape, obtain a sense of what is happening. Related lines of code, such as a list with items that wrap onto a second or third line, should be indented the same depth to indicate their relationship.

Python Programming Components

To program in Python, you need a few different components in place. Specifically, you need a computer, generally either a laptop or a desktop computer, with the following programs installed: 1) the Python interpreter, and 2) a programming environment.

The Python interpreter is the program that takes your Python code and tells the computer, or more accurately the Python **virtual machine**, what to do.

A virtual machine is a software program that mimics a hardware computer and runs inside a real computer. Running Python on a virtual machine means Python can be run regardless of the user's actual computer hardware. Running a program within a virtual machine is slower than running it directly on the machine, but it is a more flexible infrastructure. Some computers come with Python installed, but the latest stable version of Python can also be downloaded from the Python Software Foundation website.

A programming environment is where a programmer writes the actual code, typically either in a text editor or an **integrated development environment** (IDE). Text editors are programs used to write and edit plain text, such as Microsoft Notepad. Some text editors, such as Sublime Text, Vim, and Emacs, are specifically meant for writing and editing code and provide special formatting for code as well as other valuable tools.

For example, when you type a beginning set of quotation marks (", sometimes called open quotes), some text editors will automatically add a second set of quotation marks (", sometimes called close quotes). If a program had a set of open quotes that didn't have a corresponding set of close quotes, an error would occur. Thus, by automatically inserting the close quotes, the text editor helps programmers avoid errors in their code. Text editors often also apply different colors to different types of code to make it easier to quickly scan and understand the in-progress program.

An IDE includes both a place to write and edit code as well as some automation tools and code debugging tools. The default IDE for Python is IDLE, which comes with an interactive console for running, testing, and editing code as you program. PyCharm is a popular open-source alternative.

After program code is written in a text editor or IDE, that code is saved as a Python source-code file, or module, with a .py extension (just as a Microsoft Word file ends with .docx). The module (the .py file) can then be **executed** (run) in the Python interpreter.

Collections of modules with related functionality are called packages. There are thousands of modules and packages that programmers around the world have created and made available for use posted online in the Python Package Index. Using these open-source (free to use, modify, and share) modules and packages in a program can make the overall development process easier and more efficient.

Syntax

Now that we've covered the high-level organizational structure of Python code files, let's look closely at the structure of the code itself, starting with its syntax. The syntax of a language is the way that linguistic elements are put together to create meaningful sentences. The English language has syntax, and if you're reading this book you likely understand it quite well without thinking about it. Consider the following sentences:

1. A bird sang outside my window.
2. A sang my window bird outside.
3. A window sang outside my bird.

Sentence one makes sense because its syntax is accurate. If a friend told you, "A bird sang outside my window," you would know exactly what they meant. Sentence two has completely inaccurate syntax. If someone said this to you, you would likely be very confused and you'd try to rearrange the words to make sense. In both human languages and in programming languages, there are rules that determine which parts of a sentence (such as nouns and verbs) go in which order. In trying to rearrange your friend's gibberish, you'd be attempting to apply these basic rules of syntax.

Sentence three is a little trickier. It sounds somewhat correct if you don't pay attention to the words very carefully. But if someone said this to you you'd likely say, "Oh, you mean a *bird* sang outside your *window!*" Even though bird and window are both nouns, according to English syntax rules, the noun "bird" must go in front of the verb "sang" to accurately describe what happened.

An example of incorrect syntax in English is "A window sang outside my bird." Programmers must learn each coding language's syntax.

Python has a very specific syntax. We won't cover all of the elements of Python syntax in this book, but we will take a look at a few of the basic "parts of speech" within Python. If you're interested in learning Python fully, both the final chapter and the Further Information section at the back of this book contain suggestions for how to get started.

Object-Oriented Code

Python is an **object-oriented programming** language, which means that the language is more focused on data than it is on programming logic. Real world ideas are represented as objects. A person might be an object in a program, such as hotel_guest_1 in a hotel software program, as might be a building or a car. Each object has a set of properties, such as name or address, and a set of functions called **methods** that can be applied to that object.

Objects belong to **classes**. Classes are given definitions that contain the set of attributes that an object of that class can have, such as **class variables** and **instance variables**, as well as methods.

Class variables apply to all objects in a class, such as a class that represents dogs. All dogs have certain properties, such as four legs, a tail, a bark, and a name. They're all also members of the canine family. These are examples of class variables. Meanwhile, instance variables apply only to a unique instance. An instance is an individual object, such as a dog named Fido that belongs to the larger class Dog. Fido's instance variables could include his home address, his age, his latest vaccination date, and his owner's name.

Classes also have defined methods, which are special types of functions that can be associated with an object. Functions are chunks of code that can take in data and return a result. Once a function is defined, it

Objects within a class share common properties but can also vary one to another, just as all dogs have similar properties but also unique attributes.

can be used repeatedly throughout and across programs. For example, if there is a defined method called bark that tells objects of class Dog to bark, we could make Fido bark by writing "Fido.bark." We could make a dog named Rover bark by writing "Rover.bark."

Strings

Series of characters such as 'Fido' or "It's as easy as 1, 2, 3," are a very common data type called strings. A string can have single or double sets of quotation marks, but a string must start and end with the same choice of quotation marks. Three sets of single or double quotation marks indicate a string that spans more than one line, such as:

> """"Hey diddle diddle,
> the cat and the fiddle,
> the cow jumped over the moon."""

Strings are useful when you need to display text on a webpage or as part of an application. For example, a string might be used to create a display message such as, "You have reached your account limit!" or a prompt such as, "Enter a four-digit password."

Using the string data type tells the program that the characters are going to be displayed or stored and that the program shouldn't attempt to process them as program instructions. After all, using the above example, it's the user who is being told to enter a four-digit password, not the computer program! Using quotation marks indicates that difference.

Variables

The goal of a computer program is usually to model the real world. An electronic medical record, for example, electronically models a patient's real-life journey through the hospital system. A customer relationship management application electronically models the status and timeline of relationships between a salesperson and clients. The more a program mimics the real world, the more useful the program will be and the more seamless it will be to use. One way to create parity between the real world and the

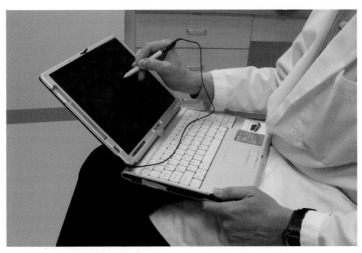

Complicated software like an electronic medical record (EMR) requires many variables.

computer-programming world is through the use of variables (also called "names" in Python).

You might have a group of friends, one of whom is your best friend. Describing your friends in conversation might sound something like this: "My closest friends are Alex, Danielle, and Sophia, and my absolute best friend is Sam." In Python, you could represent the same information (also called data) with the following:

```
friend_one = "Alex"
friend_two = "Danielle"
friend_three = "Sophia"
best_friend = "Sam"
```

Now the program knows the names of your friends and that your best friend is Sam. In the program, your friends are variables. It's generally best to use variables that are easy to remember and to understand when reviewing code. f1 = "Alex" and friend_one = "Alex" can both achieve the same end goal, but one variable name is easier to read and comprehend right away.

Numbers

There are two major numeric types in Python. Integers are whole numbers like 1, 2, 3 and -1, -2, -3. Floating-point numbers are numbers with digits after the decimal point, such as 1.2, 100.5, and -5.7. (There is also a third numeric type called complex numbers that have a real and an imaginary component, which is useful if you're working with imaginary numbers.)

Python is very good at mathematics. To multiply five and three using Python, for example, simply enter 5 * 3. This is a simple example, but Python can compute much larger problems as well.

In Python, +, -, *, and / are called **operators** because they perform addition, subtraction, multiplication, and division operations. Schoolteachers often use the acronym PEMDAS or the mnemonic "Please Excuse My Dear Aunt Sally" to teach the order of operations, or the order in which mathematical **expressions** are evaluated. PEMDAS stand for Parentheses, Exponents, Multiplication, Division, Addition, Subtraction. An expression is a combination of values, such as variables, and operators that will be evaluated. Python uses the same order of operations. In the mathematical expression (5+2) * 2, for example, the parentheses are evaluated first before the multiplication for a result of 14.

Everyday Applications

As a general-purpose programming language, Python is used in a variety of everyday contexts ranging from building web applications to conducting data science to crunching data sets in an academic environment. We touched briefly on these uses while describing the evolution of Python above. Here, we'll go into more detail.

Web Development

Python has been used to build many popular web applications including YouTube. YouTube is owned by Google, which uses Python extensively for research and to build its web applications. Other popular web applications built using Python include:

- Dropbox, the **cloud**-based storage product used to store documents, photos, videos, and more
- SurveyMonkey, the online survey provider
- Reddit, the popular news and commenting site
- Pinterest, the site where users post pictures and create interest-based image collections
- *The Onion*, the satirical newspaper
- Instagram, the popular picture- and video-based social media app
- Spotify, the music streaming service

Data Science

Python has several high-quality packages that support data science, including:

- SciPy, used for scientific and technical computing

Instagram has more than 400 million daily active users. The social media platform was built using Python.

- pandas, used for data manipulation and analysis
- matplotlib, used to generate data plots and charts
- NumPy, used for scientific computing, especially large multi-dimensional arrays

Many well-known businesses use Python for data science. As an example, let's look at Airbnb. Airbnb is a vacation-rental platform that connects travelers and homeowners (or renters) who have a room or entire house available for booking. There is a massive amount of data involved, from a vacation-rental listing's properties (number of bedrooms, available appliances, proximity to city center) to numbers of bookings to prices of listings. Analyzing these data, finding relations between them, and building models for predicting outcomes can help Airbnb provide a more enjoyable, safe, and profitable service.

Today, Airbnb uses Python, among other programming languages, to conduct data science in numerous ways. For example, Airbnb's data scientists work with the platform's large data sets in order to find trends, improve search-ranking features, create new vacation-rental pricing models, build programs that predict the quality of guest experiences, and create programs that detect risky user behaviors on the Airbnb site.

There are several other languages that are well suited for data science (such as MATLAB and R), but one advantage Python holds is that it is a general-purpose programming language. In addition to doing the analysis of the data, Python can be used to connect and build the structures around that data, such as a web application or APIs.

For-profit companies are not alone in conducting data science. Scientists use data science for the sake of knowing more about their data and the phenomena those data represent. The daily work of scientists typically includes observing natural or artificial phenomena and recording many observations. Throughout years of conducting a single research project, a scientist will gather a vast numbers of data points.

NASA's Chandra X-ray Observatory, for example, moves in an elliptical orbit far above Earth. Chandra includes an X-ray telescope that focuses X-rays from celestial objects, instruments to record those X-rays for production and analysis, and the instrumentation of the observatory itself. Chandra was launched in 1999 and is still the most sophisticated X-ray observatory.

Chandra not only records X-rays of phenomena like dying stars, it also records data about its own components. It sends that data back to astrophysicists at NASA who use it to monitor and optimize the spacecraft from afar. One important task for NASA scientists is to keep Chandra cool enough to prevent damage to the spacecraft. Typically, telescopes like Chandra have sunshields and other design features that ensure the delicate equipment is protected from

Earth's atmosphere absorbs X-rays, so Chandra orbits beyond it at an altitude of 86,500 miles (139,000 km).

Connecting the Dots

○ ○ ○

APIs are powerful tools for web-based programmers. An API is essentially a set of specifications that determines how one application can send and receive data to and from another application. An API, such as Instagram's API or Google Maps' API, typically describes the available functionality, terms of use, and the types of input or output the API supports. These two-way communication channels are important in the modern internet, and they are everywhere.

Often, when a developer or team creates a new web product, the ability to retrieve or send data from a popular application is important if not fundamental to the new product. For example, when you look at a Google Map in Yelp to see nearby restaurants, Yelp is using the Google Maps API to create that map. (It's much easier to integrate with Google Maps than to build a map application from scratch!) If you shared a news article you liked on Twitter directly from the news site, the news site used the Twitter API to offer you that streamlined option. (It benefits the news site if you share their content on Twitter!)

APIs can be built using a variety of languages and frameworks. For example, the Python-based Flask and Django web frameworks are popular choices for API development. Other common options include the Ruby-based Rails and Sinatra frameworks, Node.js, and PHP.

the sun. As both Chandra and the sun are in motion, however, that requires carefully calibrating Chandra's trajectory through space.

NASA scientists first tried using simple thermal models to control Chandra and optimize its temperature, but those models didn't work adequately to protect Chandra. In 2007, a group of scientists and engineers worked together to create more accurate thermal models. They chose to use Python this time around because of its ease of use; interactive analysis environment; and the NumPy, IPython, matplotlib, and SciPy modules and other packages created by outside companies.

A composite (combined) image of hot, young stars energizing cooler gas clouds created using data from Chandra X-ray Observatory and other sources

Eve Online

○ ○ ○

One unusual use—and one of the largest uses—of Python is the massively multi-player online game EVE Online. EVE takes place in a cluster of stars in a galaxy far away from Earth. Humans arrived through a wormhole that connected the two galaxies. Eventually, the wormhole collapsed and the colonists were cut off from other humans. Many colonies collapsed while a few survived and rose to control the EVE empires. New human races emerged in this isolated bubble of humanity.

In EVE, players interact with other characters, form military alliances, train to gain skills, and fight for survival. All players inhabit a single universe. EVE handles huge amounts of traffic at a time: the game has hundreds of thousands of players, and at peak moments, there have been more than fifty thousand people online playing EVE at the same time.

An Icelandic company called CCP developed EVE using an implementation of Python called Stackless. Stackless has higher performance (meaning it can handle more users and maintain speed and stability) than the traditional implementation of Python. Stackless's biggest differentiator compared to traditional Python is an improved **thread** structure.

The "brain" of a computer is the CPU, or central processing unit. CPUs execute the instructions of computations from computer programs. Each series of instructions is considered a "thread of execution." A traditional computer process has a single thread, which means that one set of instructions can be carried out at a time. A single-threaded application is somewhat similar to sharing a book with a friend. Only one person can read the book at a time, though you can take turns if you want to read the book together.

Today, some processes can have multiple threads (called **multithreading**) that can divide the instructions to be carried out and run them more efficiently. If one thread is busy carrying out a set of instructions, another thread can carry out a separate set of instructions without waiting for the first thread to finish. This is especially useful when one thread is blocked or running slowly.

Multithreaded structure has both advantages and drawbacks. It allows different functions to execute independently of one another, such that a failure of one function to complete or a slow execution does not affect the success of another function. However, in computer systems, each thread has its own stack, which is an allocated region of memory. When a function is executed, it adds some data to the stack, and when it completes, it removes that data from the stack. In multithreaded structures that can create high memory requirements.

Stackless is designed to harness the efficiency benefits of multithreading while using less memory. Instead of using traditional threads. Stackless relies on microthreads that can spawn small tasks called tasklets that use less memory and fewer system resources.

Memory and resources are finite and can limit the scope of a program. However, because of its lightweight architecture, Stackless allows a program like EVE to have a massive number of tasklets. The model greatly increases the capacity for **concurrency** (two or more things happening at the same time) and makes the huge multi-player game possible.

Chapter Three

Strengths and Weaknesses

Many programming languages achieve the same end goals. From an end user's perspective, there's little that would indicate that Dropbox is built using Python, while Twitter is built using Scala. Both Dropbox and Twitter are web applications with large amounts of data, multimedia, and user interaction.

In fact, Twitter was first built using Ruby and the Ruby-specific Rails web development framework and later moved to Scala. The app itself stayed largely the same. When it comes to **back-end** languages like Python, what matters is how easy and enjoyable it is to

Opposite: Twitter has about 328 million monthly active users. Its traffic peaks required moving to Scala, a fast, robust language.

program in the language, how closely the language can model thoughts and ideas, and how well the language performs when a program is executed. The back end of an application is the unseen side that deals with business logic and databases instead of the **front end** or user interface.

There isn't a specific set of characteristics that define how well a program performs, but when programmers discuss performance, they generally refer to a combination of factors including how fast a program runs, how fast it responds to user requests, and how stable it is in production (for example, does it crash?). Performance can also include factors such as how scalable a product is and how efficiently it uses resources like CPU and memory. Twitter, for example, migrated its back end to Scala because with its Ruby on Rails architecture, Twitter could not handle peak usage levels without crashing or slowing down significantly.

Python has advantages over many languages in regard to the programming experience and the structure of the language. It also lags behind other languages in certain areas, including performance.

Python Strengths

What makes Python a good language to learn and use? If you ask a Python programmer that question, you'll get a range of answers from the language's ease of use to the ability to rapidly prototype applications. You'll hear about the number of useful modules in the standard library and high quality **third-party** modules ready for use. Many also enjoy using Python because of its active, positive, open-source programming community.

Ease of Use

Every Python programmer has a unique explanation for why they chose Python as their language of choice, but a common explanation is the clean syntax and ease of learning Python. This sentiment is clearly described in an article written in the *Linux Journal* by Eric Raymond.

Raymond is a software developer who knows how to program in more than two dozen programming languages. He's also the author of a well-known book on open-source software called *The Cathedral & the Bazaar*. Raymond describes the first time he began to build a program in Python (emphasis his own):

Eric Raymond is the cofounder of a nonprofit that promotes open-source software.

I was generating *working* code nearly as fast as I could type … When you're writing working code nearly as fast as you can type and your misstep rate is near zero, it generally means you've achieved mastery of the language. But that didn't make sense, because it was still day one and I was regularly pausing to look up new language and library features! That was my first clue that, in Python, I was actually dealing with an exceptionally good design.

Compared to languages like C, Python code is extremely readable and easy to learn and work with as a beginner. This is a big advantage for the language because it draws in many beginning programmers who are happy to study Python and are validated by their quick progress.

Batteries Included

One of the design philosophies that guides Python is "batteries included." The philosophy's name is a reference to the experience of purchasing a new electronic device. It's a lot more satisfying when the device comes with everything it needs to operate, including batteries. (Or, in other cases, a charger.) Python is designed to be the same way: Python comes with a large and far-ranging set of packages available for use right from the start.

In many browsers, a padlock icon indicates that a webpage connection is secure and information you enter is encrypted.

For example, Python has a built-in module for Transport Layer Security encryption and peer authentication. SSL, as it's called, uses encryption to protect links between web servers and internet browsers to make sure that the data passed between a web server and an end user's browser is protected and secure. Transport Layer Security is the next generation of a similar concept called Secure Sockets Layer. The acronym stuck even when the name of the concept evolved.

If you've used the Chrome web browser, for example, properly secured websites show a green lock icon and the word "Secure" to the left of the URL. A non-secure site shows the words "Not Secure." A programmer building a web application can use Python's SSL module to get the "Secure" designation more easily than if they started from scratch.

The Last Friday

○ ○ ○

Imagine you own a cafe that hosts live music the last Friday of every month. As the owner, you want to identify the dates of those Fridays for the next year so you can book musicians. You could flip through a calendar, or you could write code to determine the last Friday of the month for a given year.

In C, that code would look like this:

```c
#include <stdio.h>
#include <stdlib.h>
int main(int c, char *v[])
{
    int days[] = {31,29,31,30,31,30,31,31,30,31,30,31};
    int m, y, w;
    if (c < 2 || (y = atoi(v[1])) <= 1700) return 1;
    days[1] -= (y % 4) || (!(y % 100) && (y % 400));
    w = y * 365 + (y - 1) / 4 - (y - 1) / 100 + (y - 1) / 400 + 6;
    for(m = 0; m < 12; m++) {
            w = (w + days[m]) % 7;
            printf("%d-%02d-%d\n", y, m + 1,
                    days[m] + (w < 5 ? -2 : 5) - w);
    }
    return 0;
}
```

In Python, it would look like this:

```python
import calendar
def last_fridays(year):
    for month in range(1, 13):
        last_friday = max(week[calendar.FRIDAY]
            for week in calendar.monthcalendar(year, month))
        print('{:4d}-{:02d}-{:02d}'.format(year, month, last_friday))
```

The two functions achieve the same result, but the Python code is noticeably simpler. Python can use English words such as "friday" and "calendar" to find the result whereas the C code is calculating the result entirely using integers and mathematics. Python also starts with a built-in function, Calendar, which significantly simplifies the programming task at hand.

These two examples, while small, are powerful illustrations of why someone might choose Python over C. The C code might execute faster, but it's faster and a lot more pleasant to write code that looks like English and comes with built-in functionality.

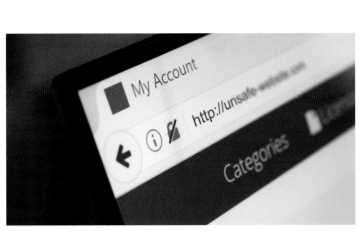

A padlock with a red strike or X indicates that a webpage connection is not secure and data you enter may be compromised.

Third-Party Libraries

In addition to the standard library of packages that come with Python, there are many third-party packages and modules available for use in Python programs. Third-party packages and modules are built by developers and made freely available for other Python users, but they have to be installed. (Installation is a very simple process, though.) In comparison, a built-in module or package is one that is included in the standard Python implementation without installation. The Python Software Foundation website curated a repository called the Python Package Index (PyPI) that includes over 100,000 packages.

One example from those 100,000-plus packages is the PyFeyn package, which simplifies the process of drawing Feynman diagrams. Physicists use Feynman diagrams to visually represent the behavior and interactions of subatomic particles such as electrons,

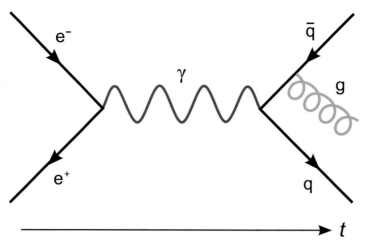

This is a Feynman diagram of the annihilation of an electron and positron, which produces a photon that decays into a quark-antiquark pair. The antiquark radiates a gluon.

photons, and quarks. The PyFeyn package makes it easier to produce a large number of diagrams. It also includes options for special effects that can make the diagrams more interesting to look at or easy to interpret.

Rapid Prototyping

Compared to other programming languages, it is easy to build a working Python program in a short amount of time. This is due in part to the ease of programming in Python and the availability of built-in packages and high quality third-party packages. For startups or others on tight timelines, this is a highly desirable feature in a programming language. Spending too much time on development before being able to launch a product can cause a startup to lose potential revenue as well as the opportunity to test their product and make quick changes to please users.

Object-Oriented Code

Object-oriented programming is just one of many programming language paradigms. It has some significant benefits, though, including that objects provide a way to closely model the real world in code. After observing the real world, a programmer can note down important nouns and the related adjectives and verbs. The nouns can be modeled with objects, grouped into classes, and given methods (available actions or verbs) and variables (descriptors or adjectives).

Other benefits of object-oriented programming include the ease of re-use, the ability to hide some code behind the scenes, and the flexibility of debugging object-oriented code. Once an object or a class is created, that same object can be reused or an object with all the properties of the class can easily be created later on in other programs. After an object is created, the code for the object itself remains hidden even when the object is used again. This "hidden" aspect makes it harder to introduce errors or accidentally modify an object once it's created. Finally, if a specific object has a bug in it, it's relatively easy to create a new bug-free object and use it in place of the buggy object.

Open-Source Community

The Python community is generally considered a welcoming community for beginners to join. The

Python Software Foundation openly encourages people from all backgrounds, orientations, and cultures to join. And the language is open-source, which means that it is free to use and distribute, even for commercial (profitable) purposes. Many of the well-known programming languages are open source, but not all. MATLAB, for example, is a proprietary programming language. It's used for numerical computing and could be considered side-by-side with Python for some uses. The fact that Python is free to use gives it an advantage in cases like these.

Perhaps more significant, however, is the spirit of many open-source software communities. Open-source communities encourage people to contribute their time to projects they are interested in to grow their own skills, make a difference in the community, and give back. By contributing to open-source projects, it's possible to work on real projects with other people in the industry and build a portfolio regardless of your employment status, age, location, or other personal factors.

Python Weaknesses

Some of Python's biggest advantages are also correlated to its weaknesses. The qualities that make Python good for rapid prototyping also introduce susceptibility to errors. Meanwhile, the simple, high-level syntax comes with a performance hit.

Ease of Mistakes

Python is a dynamically typed programming language, which means that there is no data type checking step as there would be in a statically typed language.

In a dynamically typed language, a single variable can be associated with objects of different types. For example, in a single program, the variable *friend* could be assigned to the object "Megan," which is a string data type. Later, the variable *friend* could mistakenly be assigned to the value 1, which is an integer data type.

There is no type checking performed in Python, but that does not mean that all data types work for a function. It might not work to assign a certain variable to a string, but it's possible to do so while writing the code. Because of this flexibility, incorrect data types can cause errors when the program is run.

The opposite of a dynamically typed language is a statically typed language such as Java. In a statically typed language, once the variable name *friend* was assigned to the string object "Megan" it can only be assigned to other string objects. This limits flexibility in coding, but eliminates opportunities for runtime errors (errors that occur when the program is run).

Dynamically typed languages are faster to write in because there are fewer limitations on the code. However, there is greater possibility for errors due to the lack of type checking. Recent versions of

Python 3 have a provisional Type Hints module that allows programmers to add type annotation into the code. There is still no type checking performed at runtime, however, and using the Type Hints module requires using a third-party type checker to go through and find any type-related bugs in the source code.

Flexible, fast coding comes with a tradeoff: Python is more susceptible to errors in code than stricter, slower, programming languages. As a consequence, Python programmers typically need to write **tests** to maintain confidence in the quality of their code.

In software development, tests are additional chunks of code that focus on a small piece of software functionality and prove that it behaves as intended. This process is typically called unit testing, and the tests themselves are often referred to as unit tests. Python has a built-in testing module called unittest that programmers can use to create tests for their code.

Testing is normal and expected, and using tests isn't a sign that a programming language is weak. However, in Python, it is possible to spend as much time (or more) writing tests for code as writing the code itself. Meanwhile, statically typed languages like Scala, Haskell, Rust, and Go typically require less testing to ensure the quality of program code.

Some programmers see the emergence of these statically typed languages as evidence of a shift away from the dynamically typed languages such as Python and Ruby, both of which were created in the 1990s. The fact that there are third-party type checking modules for Python and the addition of type assertions to the latest versions of Python provide even more evidence that this could be true.

Performance

The standard implementation of Python is not as fast as compiled languages such as C. Technically, most programming languages have various implementations that can be either compiled or interpreted. The standard implementation of Python is interpreted, so in this case, we will discuss Python as an interpreted language. Similarly, the standard implementation of C is compiled.

In compiled languages, the source code for a software program is converted into machine language that the computer can execute before the program is run. Compiled languages tend to be faster because when it comes time to run the program, the program is in a language the computer understands.

Python, however, is an interpreted language. In interpreted languages, the source code is not compiled into machine language in advance. Instead, an interpreter evaluates the program line-by-line into Python **bytecode**. As an analogy, consider using an

Google Translate is a useful way to read website text written in another language, but it would be slow to use in conversation!

interpreter as similar to giving a speech in a foreign language by using Google Translate to translate each sentence before you speak it. It is slow work. A compiled language, on the other hand, is like having a native speaker translate your speech for you in advance so you can give it all at once. It will be much quicker to simply read through the speech instead of stopping to translate each line!

Languages that run on the **Java Virtual Machine (JVM)**, including Java, have elements of both compiled and interpreted languages. First, the code is written in a language such as Java or Clojure or Scala. The language is then compiled from the source code into Java bytecode that is much closer to machine language. At runtime, the JVM interprets and executes the bytecode. Though there is an additional step, a JVM program is faster to run than a standard interpreted language like Python because at runtime, the program is already in an optimized format that can run very quickly.

There are implementations of Python that are very fast. PyPy, for example, achieves much greater speed than the standard Python implementation. However, the standard implementation of Python lags behind both compiled languages and JVM-based languages in execution speed.

Another performance-related area in which Python lags behind its serious competitors is in concurrency. Concurrency is the ability for a program to execute two or more series of instructions at the same time (or seemingly at the same time). Concurrency creates many complexities in programming, including the need to coordinate computing resource use between different tasks. Programmers must also ensure that the tasks running concurrently don't change data in ways that negatively affect other tasks using the same data.

As an analogy for various concurrency models, imagine you are playing a game with a group of people. Each person secretly adds a word to a sentence on a notepad and passes the notepad on to the next person. At the end, you read the sentence aloud and see what you have created together. The activity happens one piece at a time, and each person is able to review the words put on the notepad before them, so they can add a word that made sense in context.

Now imagine that halfway through the game, someone made a copy of the sentence on a second notepad and passed it in two different directions, stating that the two notepads would be combined at the end to make one sentence. Players wouldn't know what words were appearing on the other notepad, and the end result would be a mashup of words that don't make sense. This is similar to very poorly planned concurrent programming. Two series of instructions are happening at once, but the tasks are not coordinated.

A better way to play this two-notepad game would be to give half the players responsibility for the first half of the sentence and half the players responsibility for the second sentence, with a rule stating how the two halves would be joined. One half could come up with a beginning clause that ends in "because," and the second half could come up with an ending clause that gives an explanation. The game will be over in half the time, and the result will still be a funny yet coherent sentence.

The standard Python implementation can't play the optimized version of the two-notepad game. Python has a **global interpreter lock** called the GIL, which requires that a thread must hold the GIL to execute the

Disney Animation Particles

○ ○ ○

All programming languages have advantages and disadvantages. Thankfully for companies and organizations that depend on technology, programming languages can work together for a best-of-both-worlds outcome. This was true for a software program that Disney engineers created to make particle animation simpler.

The first fully animated Disney movie was *Snow White and the Seven Dwarfs*, which was released in 1937. *Snow White* and subsequent Disney films up into the 1990s were animated using illustrations that were hand-drawn and painted on transparent sheets called cels. The cels were then layered and photographed to form a composite image of a scene. Each scene was broken down into many composite images, arranged sequentially, and photographed in quick succession to create the effect of animation.

Toward the end of the twentieth century, Disney shifted to a new, modern approach using CAPS, or Computer Animation Production System. CAPS technology was created by the company Pixar, which today is famous for its own animated films. CAPS allowed the ink-and-pen-drawn scenes to be scanned into the computer and enhanced. In 1991, for example, CAPS was used to create the background for the iconic ballroom sequence in *Beauty and the Beast* in conjunction with a hand-drawn Beauty and Beast.

Today, Disney's animations use sophisticated technology to bring even the finest particles to life, such as droplets of water, snowflakes, grains of sand, and flickers of fire.

Previously, Disney animators used multiple different software products to animate particles. Using different products for the same work provided a challenge, however. Each animation system had its own proprietary particle file format, such as .pdb or .geo. A file created in one program couldn't be edited in another program. Disney's animators wanted a unified interface that could load, save, and manipulate particle files no matter what format they were saved in.

Disney's software engineers built a software library called Partio, which can read and write (modify) data from particle files of different formats. The library includes **command line** tools to look up information about a particle such as its three-dimensional coordinates, view particles, and convert particles of one format to another format. A command line is a type of computer interface in which a human interacts with a program by writing text-based commands instead of clicking or dragging screen elements around.

The Disney team built an API in C++ that allows them to manipulate massive amounts of particles at once while maintaining high performance. They built a second API in Python that makes it easy for the software developers to quickly edit particles after they've already been created. For example, if an animator needed to increase the radius of all particles in a certain region, they could use the Python API to quickly modify that single attribute.

Python could be used to manipulate massive amount of particles, but the computer would run very slowly due to Python's performance limitations, and the program could crash. C++ is better for data-intensive work because it runs much faster and can handle high workloads. However, Python is a more user-friendly language to work in, so the second API is useful for when someone wants to just add and animate a few particles at a time.

instructions it contains. (Threads, as discussed earlier, represent a series of instructions to be executed.) When a thread is finished, even if only temporarily, it releases the GIL and another thread can execute.

Thinking back to the game analogy, the GIL essentially forces Python to play the version in which each person takes their turn with the notepad one at a time. It also slows performance down because switching between threads with the GIL produces a great deal of delay. Overall, the GIL produces the desired outcome and preserves data integrity in the concurrency model, but it is slow and performance suffers.

Some of the popular JVM languages like Scala, Clojure, and Haskell have an advantage over Python here, too. Many of these languages have **immutable** data structures, which means that an object can't be modified once it is created. This greatly simplifies concurrency because data doesn't have to be locked down to preserve data integrity.

Python Use Cases

Given the ease and speed of programming in Python, Python is an especially good choice for startups that need to rapidly build and iterate on their ideas. It's also a good fit for scientists and companies with massive amounts of data given its number of data science-specific packages. It is successful in full-scale applications like Dropbox and the Instagram web application interface.

It is less ideal for situations that require high performance above all else—such as processing changes to millions of computer-animated particles. In these cases, a language like C, Java, or Scala may work better. Python's flexible, dynamic typing can also present difficulties when code needs to be maintained for long periods of time or by a large team. A language with less flexibility, such as Scala, may be a better choice in these situations.

Python is often used in conjunction with other languages and technologies that are used to create and modify databases and the front end of an application. In the next chapter, we'll discuss what those technologies are, how to get started learning Python and related skills, and the career prospects for a Python programmer. We'll also look at exciting frontiers of Python programming.

Chapter Four

Getting Started with Python

To get started with Python, it's useful to have an idea of how you learn best and what you want to do with your Python skills. It's also a good idea to consider the other technologies you might need to learn in addition to Python.

Python experts are in demand and highly paid. If you are someone who enjoys thinking about information architecture, using logic, and creatively solving real-world problems, a career in Python could be an enjoyable and rewarding path to pursue.

Learning Python

How do you learn best? Is it in a classroom environment with a teacher and other students? Or do you prefer

Opposite: Programmers must hone a variety of skills in order to succeed.

to start building a project, learning as you go? Keep the answers to these questions in mind as you explore different ways to get started learning Python.

There are many ways to learn to program in Python, from learning at home on your own time to obtaining a bachelor's or advanced degree in computer science.

Each method has its advantages and disadvantages, such as:

- Course length
- Location
- Financial cost
- Access to instructors
- Qualifications of instructors
- Accreditation of program (recognition of education quality from official organizations)
- Accountability system

It's important to pick a method that works for your individual learning style, but it's also important to remember that some methods have a greater track record of success than others.

Books

There are many books that teach Python concepts and basic computer science to complete beginners. For people who have never learned a programming language,

Learning Python is based on Mark Lutz's Python training course and contains quizzes and answers to help test knowledge retention.

popular choices include *Python Programmers for the Absolute Beginner, Learning Python,* and *Hello World! Computer Programming for Kids and Other Beginners.*

There are also many books about Python aimed at people who are already familiar with another programming language. *Learn Python the Hard Way* is a popular book among programmers who want to add Python to their repertoire. Books have the advantage of being cheap—even free if checked out from the library—ways to learn a new topic. They give you complete flexibility of location, and you can work through the book at any pace that works for you. On the other hand, there is no accountability built into learning from a book, and it's up to you to continue reading and learning.

While it is possible to learn the language by just reading about it, most programming books provide exercises for you to do on your computer as you read so you can get familiar with the code and how to build programs. Working with actual Python code is a useful way to fully grasp the concepts taught in the books.

Official Python Documentation

There is an immense amount of official documentation freely available on the official Python website. The Python Software Foundation includes a beginner's guide and a lengthy, easy-to-follow Python tutorial.

The in-depth tutorial is as comprehensive as books on the Python language. It contains many code samples throughout to illustrate each component and also has the advantage of being frequently updated to reflect changes in the language.

In addition to the Python tutorial, the Python Software Foundation website contains extensive information about available Python packages and how to use them. It describes changes to the language, such as the provisional addition of typing hints, too.

Free Online Resources

In addition to the free online documentation available on the Python Software Foundation website, there are many other free online resources for learning to program in Python.

Many websites offer free interactive coding tutorials or code challenges that provide an introduction to Python in a matter of hours. Codeacademy.com, for

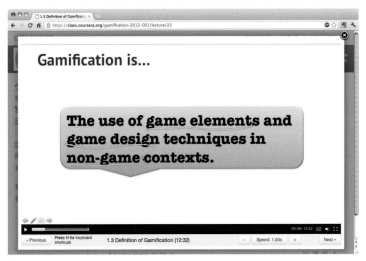

Coursera offers courses on many topics, including learning to program in Python. Here, a video lesson describes a concept that is increasingly present in apps.

example, offers a free Python course with interactive lessons instead of videos and readings. The lessons offer short pieces of instruction followed by opportunities to practice what was just learned. Another free tutorial, offered by www.learnpython.org, follows a similar format.

CodeSchool.com also offers free tutorials composed of lighthearted, Monty Python-themed instructional videos and coding challenges. Many of these online tutorial sites offer free basic lessons, while subsequent, more advanced courses require payment.

Using online tutorials to learn Python is a way to easily engage with the language. For someone who wants to simply become familiar with Python code, completing an online tutorial like the Code School course is a fun way to gain that familiarity. These tutorials alone are not enough to provide full training in Python programming, however.

A more in-depth, free, online option is a massive online open course (MOOC). MOOCs like Coursera, edX, and Udacity began in 2011 as online courses offered at no cost by well-known universities. MOOCs were intended to make high-quality education accessible to everyone, regardless of income or location. Anyone with an internet connection can enroll in a MOOC, with no admission paperwork, previous education, or experience required.

MOOCs are typically taught by professors who have adapted their courses for an online environment. The curriculum is delivered through video lessons accompanied by homework assignments and quizzes. MOOCs usually take weeks or months to complete.

One of the biggest drawbacks of MOOCs is the high dropout rate. Across the industry, the average MOOC completion rate is 15 percent. Another critique of MOOCs is that often the professors have no specific experience teaching online, and the quality of the online instruction and instructor engagement varies.

MOOCs and other online coding courses often offer "certificates of completion," but these certificates are typically not accredited by any educational oversight organization. Therefore, for people who pursue learning online, it is very important to build a portfolio of projects that can demonstrate actual skill and knowledge to potential employers.

Despite the drawbacks, MOOCs can be good tools for students with comfort using technology and a lot of discipline and self-motivation. There are no ramifications of quitting the course at any time, so it takes dedication to continue from lesson to lesson. MOOCs can also be useful for people who are looking to quickly learn the basics of a concept for a project they're working on or for an important meeting. For example, you could learn the basics of web design using a MOOC class before building your own website. A professional programmer could learn about a new technology by enrolling in a MOOC and potentially use it for future projects or to shape a new career direction.

Boot Camps

Held in the United States and around the world, programming boot camps are a relatively new way to learn programming skills. Boot camps are intensive learning programs that aim to teach a large amount of software programming skills in a concentrated, relatively short period of time.

Boot camps tend to be very project-based and often aim to teach an entire technology stack, like Python and Django.

Along with course instruction, many boot camps provide career guidance or invite companies in to see student projects. Boot camps are often held in specific locations but can also be offered online or through a hybrid approach. Boot camps require significantly more time than online courses, but that time equals valuable experience working with technology and collaborating with others on projects. Boot camps also tend to teach complementary skills like JavaScript, HTML, and CSS for web interface design or MySQL for working with databases. At the end of a boot camp, students ideally have the skills required to begin as a junior developer at a software company. According to Course Report, a company that evaluates programming boot camps, 75 percent of programming boot camp graduates find programming jobs within 120 days (approximately four months) of graduation.

Boot camps typically last about three months and include forty or more hours per week of instruction and work time. Because that time is so intensive, boot camps often take just a few months to complete, which is a great perk for anyone who needs to launch a new career quickly.

Boot camps are quite expensive however, and programs typically cost more than $10,000. (That figure doesn't include any expenses related to moving or lost income opportunities.) It's useful to remember that boot camps are for-profit companies, which means that their primary goal is to make money by selling education as a product. Boot camps are not accredited, nor are there any official standards that their teachers or courses must meet.

The high cost and accelerated timeline of boot camps make them best-suited to adults who need to quickly pivot career paths and have the flexibility of location and money for a boot camp.

Current Python boot camps include Byte Academy, which offers a variety of boot camps, from courses on full-stack software development with Python to specialized courses focused on using Python for financial technology, data science, and blockchain technology. Another, called Coding Dojo, offers a fourteen-week program that teaches Python as well as other software frameworks such as Ruby on Rails and iOS. A third, the Iron Yard, offers a Python program, as does Code Fellows and many other companies.

University Courses

According to one study, the vast majority of programming jobs (89 percent) require at least a bachelor's degree. Computer science programs teach a wide breadth of skills and foundational elements of computer science that serve programmers well. For example, computer science degrees usually involve learning more than one computer language as well as taking courses on discrete mathematics, probability,

Stanford's computer science alumni include founders, inventors, and executives of Google, Netflix, Firefox, Facebook, YouTube, Instagram, and Microsoft.

algorithms, computer systems, electronics, and more. These topics are not covered in depth in coding tutorials or coding boot camps, and having a firm grasp on the science and mathematics behind software is a strong advantage in computer science.

In addition to the core computer science courses, universities also typically have interesting courses and specializations such as **artificial intelligence (AI)**, graphics, data processing, and more. There are often opportunities to partake in research or obtain internships at successful software companies. Universities typically offer career assistance as well, from hosting job fairs to reviewing résumés and cover letters.

Compared to self-study, online courses, or a boot camp program, a four-year degree in computer science is significantly more thorough, has more resources, and includes courses taught by highly educated professors. Upon completion, students have a degree from an accredited university that attests to their credentials. University degrees can be the most expensive choice, as tuition is usually thousands or tens of thousands of dollars per year. With scholarships, however, a university education can be very inexpensive or even free.

It is possible to learn Python without going to college. Learning Python independently or through an online course or boot camp can allow programmers to begin building small applications or contributing to open source software projects. With a big-enough portfolio of work, many self-taught programmers are able to find a job or build a successful startup.

These people are typically the exception, however. Established companies with complex computing tend to require at least a bachelor's degree and often prefer higher education degrees.

For example, data science positions posted at Airbnb in 2017 required not just knowledge of Python but a four-year college degree with a master's degree or PhD preferred. A data science position posted at NASA in 2017 required "knowledge of and significant programming experience with Python" as well as **machine learning** and knowledge of additional computer programming languages. The NASA position also required a PhD in computer science, electrical engineering, or related field, or a master's degree with two years of professional experience.

Fortunately for Python fans, Python has become one of the most popular, if not the single most popular, languages taught in introductory computer science courses in the United States. Philip Guo, an assistant professor of cognitive science at the University of California, San Diego, looked at the top-ranked universities' course lists to determine the most common programming language taught in introductory courses. Of the top thirty-nine computer science programs as ranked by *US News and World Report* in 2014, Python was the most common language used in introductory computer science courses. (The second most common language used in introductory courses was Java, followed by MATLAB and C.)

Among universities, there are a few computer science departments that consistently stand out. As of April 2017, according to *US News and World Report,* the Massachusetts Institute of Technology was ranked number one among universities that offer doctoral degrees. Stanford University was in second place, followed by the University of California, Berkeley. These names are heavyweights in the realm of computer science. There are many other strong computer science departments across the United States and abroad.

Conferences

It's important for professional programmers to learn about technologies that are new to the industry or perhaps just new to them. This commonly takes place through programming conferences, such as the annual

PyCon or EuroPython or EuroSciPy. Conference talks are typically not long enough to provide a comprehensive overview of a new topic, but they can serve as introductions or provide unique perspectives.

Attending a conference is also an opportunity to meet people in the industry and network with potential employers. For those who want to establish their expertise in a field, speaking at a conference is a common way to solidify a strong reputation. Because conferences are so valuable when it comes to sparking new ideas and building connections, many software industry employers will pay for their employees to attend one or more conferences per year.

Complementary Technologies

Computer science is a field that requires expertise in many interconnected technologies. Most people who program know multiple programming languages and tools that work in harmony to produce attractive, complex, secure, and stable applications and infrastructures. For example, building a web application such as Dropbox requires multiple technologies to create the database and the user interface and to manage the communication between the two.

Web Technologies

Programmers who want to use Python for web development should learn related web technologies as well. Most web applications use jQuery, AJAX, and other JavaScript platforms for elegant, responsive front ends. Typically, most web applications also use MySQL or other database languages.

JavaScript is a programming language that was created in 1995. It typically works inside a web browser to give programmers the ability to control the elements of the user interface. A major benefit of JavaScript is that it can perform a lot of valuable functions in the browser without requiring communication from the web page to the server and back to the web page. For example, a programmer could use JavaScript to make sure that the data a user enters on a web page is correct. If someone enters "FINALLY FRIDAY!" into a date field instead of a standard date format such as 10/15/2017, JavaScript can be used to check whether the response is an allowed response. If not, the web page can display a message telling the user that the date was entered in an incorrect format. Without JavaScript, the user would have to fill out the entire form, click submit, and then learn that their responses were wrong. JavaScript can also be used to add dynamic, interactive features to web pages, such as maps that can update in real time.

While JavaScript is a very powerful tool for designing web front ends, today it's more common to use jQuery instead of traditional JavaScript. jQuery is a JavaScript library that simplifies and condenses JavaScript syntax. It is also the most widely used JavaScript library because of its ease of use and effectiveness.

Writing jQuery requires fewer lines of code than writing the same functionality in JavaScript. jQuery has a larger library of functions than other JavaScript libraries, which gives programmers more prebuilt modules to add to their applications. jQuery code works across all browsers (unlike JavaScript), makes it easy for developers to create new plug-ins, and supports AJAX templates.

AJAX stands for Asynchronous JavaScript and XML, and it provides a way for web pages and servers to communicate and exchange data. When the web page makes a request, AJAX can send the request to the server, retrieve the correct information, and update the web page without refreshing the page at any point in the process. This behavior may seem standard, but without AJAX, the website would have to be completely refreshed to display new information.

In addition to front-end technologies, it's also useful to learn technologies to manage the back end of web applications. MySQL is a common choice for managing databases. MySQL is a relational database management system used in web applications across the world, such as Facebook, Twitter, YouTube, and more. A relational database is a database that is structured in tables with rows and columns that describe the relationship between stored items. For example, a relational database for a social media application might have rows of application users and columns filled with attributes such as name, age, home city, and short bio. These relational databases are often the foundation of web applications. MySQL has a client-server model, meaning that typically the database runs on a server and the client (the browser) requests, sends, and updates information from the database.

Python web developers should also be familiar with different web frameworks, especially Django and Flask. Not all web applications built using Python are built with a web framework, but many are.

Data Science Technologies

For data science positions, it's useful to know a variety of other languages and technologies used in data science. For example, many data science positions also require knowing the statistical programming language R or the numeric computing language MATLAB. Other valuable technologies to learn include Hadoop (a Java-based programming framework that supports storing and processing extremely large data sets on computer clusters), Java, and SQL. (SQL is the industry-standard programming language for database management.) Learning data visualization and statistics will also be helpful if not required.

Git and GitHub

Professional programmers should also be familiar with Git and GitHub. Git is a version-control system that makes it easier for programmers to safely edit and collaborate on code before moving new features or bug fixes to production environments. Git allows programmers to make a copy of code to use in development, make changes to code, move development code into production, and compare past versions of code to newer versions. Git is usually used in the command line. Git integrates with GitHub, which is a web-based application.

GitHub is a repository where programmers and software companies store their code files for a project. GitHub acts as a changelog, or record, that documents all of the changes and revisions that have taken place in a project over time. It also allows for comments, questions, and bug reporting.

It's useful to learn GitHub early because GitHub often acts as a résumé for programmers. If you want to become a professional programmer, put any projects you build on GitHub, and contribute to open-source projects on GitHub as much as possible. When it comes time to look for a job, having a track record of projects and open-source contribution is valuable.

Career Prospects

Python career paths vary. You could work as a web developer at a startup or build web applications for an established enterprise software company. (Enterprise software is software built for large businesses.) You could work as a data analyst at a software company or at a business whose industry depends on data. You could tackle big research projects as a data scientist in an academic or research environment such as at NASA, or work as a software engineer, building infrastructure such as OpenStack, a cloud operating system developed jointly by Rackspace and NASA.

Regardless of the industry or sector, there are likely to be plenty of well-paid jobs available. Computer science is one of the fastest-growing industries in the country. According to the federal government's Bureau of Labor Statistics, employment of software developers is expected to grow 17 percent from 2014 to 2024. This growth rate is much faster than average.

According to data from Burning Glass Technologies, a company that analyzes job market data, there were 131,748 Python jobs posted in the United States in 2014. In 2014, the average annual salary posted for Python jobs was $104,228 compared to Objective-C's average of $105,700 and Ruby's average of $107,547. (Objective-C is the language used to build software for Apple's OS X and iOS devices.)

According to the Social Security Administration, the average wage in the United States in 2014 was $44,569. Compared to this national average, a career in Python is quite lucrative.

Future Technologies

Python is useful in some of the most exciting future technologies. For example, Python can be used in artificial intelligence (the making of intelligent computer programs) and machine learning (teaching computers to learn new concepts without explicit programming).

Artificial intelligence and machine learning are increasingly powerful and common technologies. Computers are getting rapidly smarter, and various companies are building and leveraging that intelligence for commercial purposes. Companies including

The Amazon Echo uses voice recognition to control other smart devices, place delivery orders upon request, send messages, and more.

NASA, Rackspace, and OpenStack

○ ○ ○

In 2009, NASA and Rackspace collaborated to build an open-source cloud services platform, using Python, called OpenStack. OpenStack provides cloud computing, storage, and networking resources to businesses.

The "cloud" is a common buzzword in tech news and business headlines. Using the cloud, broadly speaking, means using the internet (more specifically a network of servers) to store and access data. A network of servers can provide more storage space and computing power than a single computer could handle. (The opposite of cloud storage and computing is **local** storage and computing, which means data is stored on and accessed from a single computer's hard drive.)

Many businesses use cloud computing because the infrastructure is both logistically and financially more efficient. Amongst cloud providers, there are two major types: public and private. A public cloud, such as Amazon Web Services (AWS), uses resources from shared hardware owned and operated by a third party (such as Amazon). Public clouds are usually proprietary, which means that the service provider makes it difficult (or impossible) to move data to a competing service provider.

Private cloud services such as OpenStack, on the other hand, consist of clouds that are dedicated entirely to a single business. A private cloud user can use OpenStack at their own on-site data center or use an OpenStack service provider's data center. Regardless of where it is hosted, the cloud's computing resources are not shared with any other businesses or organizations. Private clouds are more secure than public clouds and can be more configurable to a business's needs. Some services are legally required to be stored in private clouds because they provide greater data privacy. Thus, private clouds tend to be good choices for finance, healthcare, and government organizations.

Many global corporations use OpenStack, including Best Buy, Walmart, and Volkswagen. The biggest OpenStack user, however, is CERN, the European Organization for Nuclear Research. CERN built the world's largest particle accelerator, the Large Hadron Collider (LHC). The LHC is a 17-mile (27.3 kilometer), underground circular structure that uses powerful magnets to accelerate particles to nearly the speed of light. The accelerator also contains cameras that take photos 40 million times per second during particle collisions, generating an immense amount of data. These photos provide a digital representation of the particles created in the collisions and the interactions and decay of those particles. Physicists use this information to study the fundamental laws of nature.

The LHC is located on the border of Switzerland and France, but CERN's data centers are in Geneva and Budapest. The two data centers use OpenStack for their cloud infrastructure and have a total of more than 190,000 **cores**. A core is a processing unit that can receive instructions and perform functions or computations. A single core can perform one task at a time; multiple cores can perform multiple tasks at a time.

In comparison, a standard MacBook Air laptop has two cores while a standard MacBook Pro has four cores. A researcher at CERN gains hundreds of thousands of times more computing power when accessing CERN's OpenStack distribution!

Google and Tesla have built self-driving cars that can sense traffic lanes, detect speed and direction changes in surrounding vehicles, and generally process and respond to data-rich environments. Computer programs are progressively better at recognizing people in photos, making sense of handwritten text, detecting spam email, and more. We can talk to our smartphones, and they understand us. Some of us have devices in our home like Amazon's Echo, which we can command to play music, close the blinds, and adjust the room temperature.

Much of this artificial intelligence and many of these devices (or robots) were programmed using machine learning. Sometimes, we are a part of the machine learning process when we don't know it.

Every time we tagged a friend on Facebook, for example, we taught Facebook to recognize that set of

In 2017, iRobot announced that its Roomba vacuums had been mapping home floor plans, which it hoped to sell to Amazon, Apple, or Google.

visual attributes as "Maria" or another set as "Anthony." Now, Facebook can automatically identify friends and suggest who to tag in a post. The facial recognition software Facebook uses is built on an algorithm that calculates a unique number based on metrics such as the distance between the eyes, nose, and ears.

iPhones also use machine learning to improve their voice recognition software. When someone leaves a voicemail for an iPhone 6 (or higher) user, the transcription software does its best to write down what the person said. As of April 2017, the software is still a beta (test) version, and there are often incorrectly transcribed words or blank spaces left in the transcription. At the end of the message, Apple asks whether the transcription was useful or not useful. Clicking either option helps teach the software how to do a better transcription job.

Data analysis is at the center of machine learning and artificial intelligence. Creating intelligent machines means creating machines that can sense and interpret vast amounts of data, identify meaningful patterns, and take appropriate actions. Python, with its powerful data science libraries and capabilities, is a natural fit for machine learning and artificial intelligence projects.

An open-source Python library called scikit-learn provides important tools for machine learning, including classification (determining which category an object belongs to), clustering (grouping similar objects together), and preprocessing (transforming input data such as text into data that can be used in algorithms). Spotify, for example, uses scikit-learn to develop music recommendations for its music-streaming application users. OkCupid uses scikit-learn to comb through the dating site's massive amounts of data and improve its matchmaking system.

Putting It All Together

Python is a widely useful language that is relatively simple to learn. It's been popular for decades in web development and general software development, and now its popularity is growing in data-driven fields including data science and machine learning.

Whether you'd like to learn Python to have a general understanding of computer programming or pursue Python to the extent of an advanced computer science degree, knowing how to program in Python is a valuable skill that increases the number of opportunities available to you in life.

<Glossary/>

application programming interface (API) A set of specifications for how one web application can talk to another application; APIs allow developers to incorporate third-party data and tools.

artificial intelligence (AI) The science of making intelligent computer programs and other intelligent machines.

back end The behind-the-scenes parts of a web application, including the server, application logic, and database.

bytecode Compiled code, often in a language-specific format such as Java bytecode, that is run by a virtual machine.

classes Templates for a type of objects that define attributes such as variables and methods.

class variable A variable that is shared by all instances within a class.

cloud In computer science, a metaphor that describes datacenters filled with servers. Solo developers and businesses can connect to the cloud via the internet in order to store data and run programs.

command line A simple interface that people use to interact with a program by writing text-based commands, such as "ls desktop" to list all desktop files.

compiler A software program that converts higher-level code into machine code or a lower level that a computer can read and execute.

concurrency The ability for a software program to perform multiple tasks simultaneously, such as streaming a song and saving user feedback about the song.

core In computers, a processing unit that receive instructions and perform actions based on those instructions; having more cores in a single computer typically increases computer speed.

data science The field of analyzing and manipulating data sets to find trends and insights.

execution The process of running a software program or a specific programming command.

expression A single value or combination of values connected by one or more operators that will be evaluated.

front end The part of a web application that a user sees (the user interface), typically built using HTML, CSS, and JavaScript.

function A piece of code that represents a longer set of instructions and performs a specific task.

global interpreter lock An object that prevents multiple threads from simultaneously executing Python bytecodes.

immutable Something that cannot be changed once it's created.

implementation An option for reading and executing a programming language; CPython, Jython, and PyPy are different implementations or options for running Python.

instance variable A variable that belongs to only a single instance of a class.

integrated development environment (IDE) A software application in which programmers can write code, often including tools for automation, compiling, and debugging code.

interpreter A software program that can translate and execute a computer program line by line.

Java virtual machine (JVM) A virtual machine that interprets and executes Java bytecode.

local A term that describes data storage or computation conducted on a user's hard drive.

machine learning A type of artificial intelligence in which computers are taught to learn without explicit programming.

method In object-oriented programming, the type of function that is defined in a class definition.

mnemonics Letters that help people remember something complex.

module In Python, a source file with Python code.

multithreading The use of multiple threads of control to execute tasks.

object-oriented programming A programming model that revolves around data structures instead of functions.

operator Components that manipulate values through arithmetic, comparison, logic, and more.

packages A collection of related Python modules, or source code files.

specification A programming language specification defines a programming language so that people who use that language have a shared understanding of how to read and write it.

stack In computer systems, an allocated region of memory.

statement An instruction that the Python interpreter can execute.

subroutines Commonly used chunks of code.

syntax The acceptable ways linguistic elements can be combined to create meaningful sentences.

tests Additional chunks of code that focus on a small piece of functionality and prove that it behaves as intended.

third-party In the tech world, "third-party" often describes software or hardware created to integrate with another company's technology, such as games created for Facebook by individual developers.

thread An ordered sequence of instructions for execution.

virtual machine A software program that mimics a hardware computer and runs other programs.

Books

Downey, Allen. *How to Think Like a Computer Scientist: Learning with Python 2nd Edition*. Sebastopol, CA: O'Reilly Media, 2015.

Mattes, Eric. *Python Crash Course: A Hands-On, Project-Based Introduction to Programming*. San Francisco: No Starch Press, 2015.

Sweigart, Al. *Invent Your Own Computer Games with Python*. San Francisco: No Starch Press, 2016.

Websites

Programming Foundations with Python

https://www.udacity.com/course/programming-foundations-with-python--ud036

Learn the basics of programming and Python in a free, six-week course.

Python

https://www.codecademy.com/learn/python

Learn Python concepts and practice Python programming with free interactive lessons on Code Academy.

The Python Tutorial

https://docs.python.org/3/tutorial/index.html

Learn Python syntax and best practices using well-written, easy-to-follow documentation on the official Python Software Foundation site.

Videos

"Python Programming"

https://www.youtube.com/watch?v=N4mEzFDjqtA

This Python introductory video demonstrates the nuts and bolts of writing Python, starting with the very first steps of installing Python and a Python IDE.

"So You Want to Be a Full-stack Developer? How to Build a Full-stack Python Web Application."

http://pyvideo.org/pycon-us-2014/so-you-want-to-be-a-full-stack-developer-how-to.html

Learn about the components of a Python web application, including the operating system, web server, and database, as well as configuring a local development environment and deployment.

Brooks, Ashley. "14 Best Programming Languages Based on Earnings & Opportunities." Rasmussen College, May 4, 2015. http://www.rasmussen.edu/degrees/technology/blog/best-programming-languages-based-on-earnings-and-opportunities/.

Da Cruz, Frank. "Programming the ENIAC." Columbia University Computing History, April 24, 2017. http://www.columbia.edu/cu/computinghistory/eniac.html.

Disney. "Partio." Retrieved April 24, 2017. https://www.disneyanimation.com/technology/partio.html.

Eggleston, Liz. "What Is a Coding Bootcamp?" Course Report, March 28, 2017. https://www.coursereport.com/coding-bootcamp-ultimate-guide.

Fairhurst, Gorry. "Example of Assembly." Retrieved May 15, 2017. http://www.erg.abdn.ac.uk/users/gorry/eg2069/assembly.html.

Guo, Philip. "Python Is Now the Most Popular Introductory Teaching Language at Top U.S. Universities." July 7, 2014. https://cacm.acm.org/blogs/blog-cacm/176450-python-is-now-the-most-popular-introductory-teaching-language-at-top-u-s-universities/fulltext.

Jordan, Katy. "MOOC Completion Rates: The Data." June 12, 2015. http://www.katyjordan.com/MOOCproject.html.

Moreira, Belmiro. "Unveiling CERN Cloud Architecture."
Retrieved April 27, 2017. https://www.openstack.org/
videos/tokyo-2015/unveiling-cern-cloud-architecture.

Oracle. "What Is an Object?" Retrieved April 24, 2017. https://
docs.oracle.com/javase/tutorial/java/concepts/object.html.

Pemberton, Steven. "The ABC Programming Language: A Short
Introduction." February 22, 2012. http://homepages.cwi.
nl/~steven/abc/.

Peters, Tim. "Pep 20 — The Zen of Python." Python Software
Foundation, August 22, 2004. https://www.python.org/dev/
peps/pep-0020/.

Python Software Foundation. "Classes." Retrieved April 24,
2017. https://docs.python.org/3/tutorial/classes.html.

———. "General Python FAQ." Retrieved April 24, 2017.
https://docs.python.org/3/faq/general.html#why-was-
python-created-in-the-first-place.

———. "The Python Tutorial." Retrieved April 24, 2017. https://
docs.python.org/3/tutorial/index.html.

Raymond, Eric. "Why Python?" *Linux Journal*, April 30, 2000.
http://www.linuxjournal.com/article/3882.

Rouse, Margaret. "Object-Oriented Programming (OOP)."
TechTarget, August 2008. http://searchmicroservices.
techtarget.com/definition/object-oriented-programming-
OOP.

Sande, Warren. *Hello World: Computer Programming for Kids and Other Beginners*. Greenwich, Connecticut: Manning Publications, 2013.

Time. "Fifty Years of BASIC, the Programming Language that Made Computers Personal." April 28, 2014. http://time.com/69316/basic/.

Van Rossum, Guido. "King's Day Speech." *Neopythonic*, April 27, 2016. http://neopythonic.blogspot.com/2016/04/kings-day-speech.html.

———. "Personal History – Part 1, CWI." The History of Python, January 20, 2009. http://python-history.blogspot.com/2009/01/personal-history-part-1-cwi.html.

———. "Python's Design Philosophy." The History of Python, January 13, 2009. http://python-history.blogspot.com/2009/01/pythons-design-philosophy.html.

Van Rossum, Guido, Barry Warsaw, and Nick Coghlan. "PEP 8 – Style Guide for Python Code." Python Software Foundation, August 1, 2013. https://www.python.org/dev/peps/pep-0008/.

United States Department of Labor."Software Developers." Occupational Outlook Handbook. December 17, 2015. https://www.bls.gov/ooh/computer-and-information-technology/software-developers.htm.

Van Rossum, Guido, Jukka Lehtosalo, and Lukasz Langa. "PEP 484 – Type Hints." *Python Software Foundation*. May 22, 2015. https://www.python.org/dev/peps/pep-0484/.

Rachel Keranen is a writer based in Madison, Wisconsin. Her work focuses on science, software, and entrepreneurship. She's passionate about learning and loves taking deep dives into science and software. In addition to the books that she writes for Cavendish Square, such as *The Power of Ruby* and *The Composition of the Universe: The Evolution of Stars and Galaxies*, Keranen's previous work includes articles in the *Minneapolis/St. Paul Business Journal* and the *London Business Matters* magazine. Keranen enjoys traveling, biking, and spending time near water.